TRANSTRÖMER INTERNATIONAL

An Intercontinental Perspective
on the Poetry of
Nobel Laureate Tomas Tranströmer

Dracopis Press

Tranströmer
International

—edited by—
Kristian Carlsson

CREDITS & ACKNOWLEDGMENTS

Preface by Kristian Carlsson.

I. Tranströmer Triangulated
Edited by Kristian Carlsson from the recordings of a live event.
Original content by Kristian Carlsson, Ángela García, Azita Ghahreman,
Anisur Rahman, Tomas Tranströmer.
Translations of Ángela García & Tomas Tranströmer by Kristian Carlsson.

II. Tranströmer out of Language
Curated by Kristian Carlsson.
Original poems by Tomas Tranströmer.
Published in agreement with Tomas Tranströmer.
Annotations by Kristian Carlsson.
Translations of Tomas Tranströmer by Nimao Ahmed Bulaleh, Kristian Carlsson,
Ángela García, Azita Ghahreman, Juri Gurman, Iren Horvatne, Jamal Jumá,
Simon Marainen, Sohrab Rahimi, Anisur Rahman, Hikaru Sugi, Lasse Söderberg.
Additional language working group: James Brewster, Lidia Elfstrand, Bile Hashi,
Thomas Marainen, Freke Räihä.
Original Tranströmer poems have been selected by: Anisur Rahman for the
Bengali poem; Azita Ghahreman for the Farsi poem; Ángela García for the
Spanish poems; Hikaru Sugi and Kristian Carlsson for the haiku poems;
Kristian Carlsson for all other translations.

III. In Case of Inspiration from Tranströmer
Edited by Kristian Carlsson.
Original poems by Kristian Carlsson, Ángela García, Azita Ghahreman,
Anisur Rahman.
Annotations by Kristian Carlsson.
Translations by Kristian Carlsson, Maura Dooley, Ángela García, Elhum Shakerifar.

Dracopis_001
Tranströmer International; An Intercontinental Perspective on
the Poetry of Nobel Laureate Tomas Tranströmer

2013: EUROPE / HARDCOVER   ISBN 978-91-87341-00-7
2013: USA / SOFTCOVER   ISBN 978-91-87341-01-4

Published by Dracopis Press, Sweden
beard@dracopis.com   www.dracopis.com

Tomas Tranströmer was awarded the Nobel Prize in Literature 2011. He was then the first Swedish writer to become a laureate for almost forty years. And during those years Tranströmer also has been the only Swede commonly regarded to be worthy of the prize. Albeit three Swedes—and six fellow Scandinavians—were awarded the prize during the first forty years of its existence, some noticeable changes in approach have occurred over time. There might be a lot to be said about the limited origin of laureates—predominated by Western Europe and the U.S.; but, as one can see, no longer by Swedish writers. None the less, choices are made, and the static list of laureates is an annually expanded retrospective. Though, in time awarded writers might wander into oblivion. But for the time being Tomas Tranströmer—among others—must be relevant, also to an international extent.

There's little intention for this anthology to explain or investigate why Tranströmer was awarded the Nobel Prize. We take upon us a perhaps more challenging focus: How is his poetry perceived in continents predominated by other literary preferences? And in addition to that: The literal appearance of his poetry in essentially different languages.

Although relatively consistent in his imagery and distinctiveness, Tomas Tranströmer, born in 1931, has undertaken a literary journey loosely connected to the predominant syles of each era since his debut: from the trademarked European modernist poetry of the 50's and 60's, to the politically oriented poetry of the 60's and 70's, the naturalist and somewhat folkloric poetry of the 70's and the 80's, and further on to the concise and contemplative poetry of the 80's and 90's. Predominately publishing himself as a haiku poet in the 00's, might be regarded as an elliptical follow up to his haikus of the late 50's (which remained unpublished for decades). Having suffered a stroke in 1990, Tranströmer met with continuous challenges in everyday life, and the expectations for the continuation of his literary work have been consequently altered. Anisur Rahman, one of the participants in this anthology, recalls a conversation from one of the times he met with Tomas Tranströmer, in which Monica, his wife, explained: "Tomas had many ambitions and plans to write other collections of poetry, with further dimensions of his literary world."

Due to the world politics of the last decades, a diverse set of new exile writers enrich Swedish literature. Thus dictatorial governments have unintentionally contributed to Sweden being better equipped with influences to achieve literary diversity nowadays, than when Tranströmer had his debut in the 50's. Exiled writers, dissident writers, refugees becoming writers, forthcoming writers born in exile, and so on. Instead of being unconditionally westernized, Swedish literature might soon finally break free from colonial domination (although not territorially colonized, the intellectual supremacy has been thoroughly contaminated in Sweden as well). The translations in this anthology show samples of the vast smorgasbord of literary talent that enables a multilingual voice for poets like Tranströmer across the continents. And some writers who are the focal point of other hemispheres can—in that context—shed some light on Swedish poetry. Such as when we in August 2012 performed the live session that is the basis of this anthology, and BBC Persian had a film crew take a detour to Malmö in order to hear the Iranian poet Azita Ghahreman express her views on Tranströmer (the feature is available on the Web). And the Colombian poet Ángela García has been invited to express her opinion on Tranströmer across the Hispanic parts of the world.

Prospects have also arisen, allowing to fill in the gaps of the translated Tranströmer—already available in some sixty languages, he hereby can also be read in Somali (curiously, this Cushitic-branched Afro-Asiatic language didn't get its official character set for script until in 1972); and in Romani (characteristically, this now predominantly European Sanskrit-descended Indo-Aryan language has ample relatives, such as Hindustani, Bengali and Punjabi). There is a lot to be said about language, from time to time, not to forget that languages can be the apt refuge from exile of literary creativity.

Although this anthology undeniably concerns the poetry of Tomas Tranströmer, in parts it is more a statement of language. Language by definition includes as well as excludes. Being its reader, you will basically always be excluded from something in this book, in terms of understanding the language, even knowing the character set. Linguistically the pages of this book travel the continents, by body and soul.

To ensure some final amount of transgression on the literature, the main contributors to this project represent themselves in poetry inspired by Tranströmer. Being a poet, the process of translating another poet into one's mother tongue renders inscrutable insights into the process of writing and into the different facets of a poet—through the use of one's own words.

Kristian Carlsson, editor etc.

TRANSTRÖMER TRIANGULATED

The seminar of Tranströmer International—
by selected World Poets inhabiting Sweden:
Ángela García, originated from Colombia,
Azita Ghahreman, originated from Iran,
Anisur Rahman, originated from Bangladesh;
moderated by Kristian Carlsson.

AZITA GHAHREMAN: Quite a few years ago, perhaps ten or so, Sohrab Rahimi had started to translate the poems of Tomas Tranströmer into Farsi—and when the good news was announced, that Tranströmer would get the Nobel Prize of 2011, Sorhab and I agreed on making an addition to those translations together, in order to publish a book in Iran. We made a selection from all of his books and added an introduction to his world of thoughts and world of poetry, to give some guidance for the Iranian reader on what one can expect to find is his literary domains. As we decided to get the book published in Iran, we faced a lot of problems—we never got printing permission by the Iranian Government; we changed publisher several times to apply over and over again, but it never worked out well with the authorities and we never got any suitable solution out of it. Finally, after a year of efforts with the censorship, we decided to have the book published in Norway instead.

During our work we found the following words central to Tranströmer's poetics—used as metaphors, images, and model:

"Darkness", "Sun", "I" (as in the self), "Death", "Journey". And the "Way", the "Path", is something that holds a special position in his poems.

All of these words form and paint his special world. As Tranströmer once said in an interview about his poems:

"Two subjects are central to the topics in my poems: The Journey and the Death."

When the reporter asked him why it is so, he replied:

"I think all of the things on Earth are in a state of change and transformation. And at the end of all of the roads and all of the changes, death is waiting."

The nature in his poetry functions as a main character as well, a live person who performs through the words. Tranströmer uses the nature and covers everything we can see around us: snow, rain, mountains, rivers, islands. He covers nature by metaphore, and the same science he has got in his mind. Alltogether this method becomes a true sentence, in which he shows and introduces his world.

In another interview he was asked why his poems refer to mythology and religion, to ancient legends and stories. Tranströmer then explained:

"I use mythology as a metaphor."

Mythology has a powerful energy and is a good source to Swedish culture. And by reminding his readers about the mythology he builds the poetry around common knowledge.

KRISTIAN CARLSSON: Talking about mythology as metaphors, I think it might perhaps be something that makes him likable in Iran, for instance. Because when it comes to your own poetry, although different, you often use mythology; you use the mythology of the Bible since you can't use the mythology of the Quran—and in that sense you also use mythology as a metaphor. And it is somewhat like that in poetry in general in present time Iran...

AZITA GHAHREMAN: When there is a source of common knowledge, all of the people can find understanding of the metaphor through the legends. I have used this method, and in Iran it is commonly used by poets to describe what we aren't allowed to mention. If I was to compare Tranströmer to the Persian poetry, I must say they are completely different. Mysticism is the basis of Persian poetry since ancient times. And in Iran there's a long tradition of using poetry as protest, as a protest against the current situation at different times—thus the poems are so colorful and emotional. Tranströmer doesn't show his feelings by sentimentalism or melodramatic tendencies. He is spreading his images over the poems one by one in a fixed rhythm, since he has a good knowledge about music; but not about the turmoil of riots and protests. The structure of his poems is very different to ours, and when we read his poems we note the sense of logical methodology in every sentence and every word. Furthermore we note the absence of eroticism and strong passion. But that also makes him special to us. For this matter, I think his books would interest a Persian reader.

KRISTIAN CARLSSON: Maybe that's something typical for the poem "C-Dur", which is included in Farsi in this anthology. Tranströmer avoids placing the strong emotions within the time span of the poem, which in fact can be said to take place *after* the emotions. The storyline of "C-Dur" is enacted *after* making love, after leaving the apartment of one's lover.

ÁNGELA GARCÍA: I wonder about what other poets of your generation think of Tranströmer's poetry.

AZITA GHAHREMAN: The first poetry collection of Tranströmer in Farsi came in 2002—but that one was published in Sweden, and it took several years for it to be distributed in Iran. When he was discovered by my generation, poets born in the sixties, it was to a great liking. And even more so, the younger generations are familiar with modern poetry; which started to spread only fifty years ago. Now we can find a lot of common ground with some of Tranströmer's poems.

ANISUR RAHMAN: I find Tranströmer a lot more political. He was once asked about the political involvement in his poetry. And explained that in a word all his writings are the collected works of his experience of everything. I find that, although his politics can't be seen, he was indirectly political—that's why his poetry is so powerful. And mysticism is one thing that shows its power through poetry, that is: Tranströmer could show us the fundamental way of living by passing on experiences from previous generations. As when he writes about the old time farmer ploughing the fields. You can discover his politics in images and metaphors. And you'll find his emotions in the metaphors.

AZITA GHAHREMAN: I can see the same things, but by that I still find a crucial difference in contast to openly political writings. He doesn't talk about politics and Swedish society like a journalist or an activist. He lives under a different kind of pressure in Sweden than you do in dictatorships, and doing so he must describe his society in another way than we. But of course he has his methods: he talks about loneliness, and the struggle to find truth on Earth. That becomes political since he doesn't give a full explanation of things—as a reader you have to put your own values into his words. The same kind of restrictiveness we have known as political in Iran, due to censorship. But sometimes he's too avoiding of conflict. He never shows an example of fighting or protests. Maybe this is what makes him resemble a Zen Buddhist in his writings.

ÁNGELA GARCÍA: Due to the political situation in Latin America Tranströmer didn't get an easy start there. One has to reflect upon how he found his way into our lives, and how my generation received him. We could hardly even attempt to understand the poetical world of Tranströmer when we first got to know it. In Colombia in the nineties we experienced a state of constant fear due to the elevated war between drug cartels, the paramilitary and guerilla fractions. I now remind myself of the cruelty of the Latin American dictatorships we had to struggle against. We were by necessity very political, and still are. We were drawn to poets and writers that could interpret our life changing quest for independence, our rage and disgust facing the sudden disappearance of thousands of citizens, and our energetic resistance against oppression, corruption; and the exemptions from punishment.

The most humane poets were the revolutionary ones, and amongst them several Cubans—we also read poets like Roque

Dalton from El Salvador, Allen Ginsberg from the U.S., Nazim Hikmet from Turkey, Mayakovsky from Russia, and of course Pablo Neruda, from Chile. Quite a lot of the contemporary poets in Latin America even had dissociated themself from the Mexican poet Octavio Paz, since he wasn't politically oriented to the Left.

Initially Tranströmer was translated for an edition to be published in Spain, but later on he was introduced in domestic publications as well. Although he was present among the other Swedish poets that I came in contact with in anthologies, it was during the eighties Tranströmer finally became more widely translated and introduced in Latin America. I think it was due to a literary festival in 1981 when Tranströmer also visited Latin America for the first time, by invitation from the Mexican poet Homero Aridjis.

A man like Tranströmer, who on his part observes such an idyllic pasture—at first had little impact on us: did it have anything at all to do with our lives? In what way could it benefit our revolutions? In what way could it benefit our longing to establish human rights in a society that were in need to be rebuilt? We tried to find answers in any letter of his that could be an attempt to recognize the collective movement. Tomas Tranströmer gave us beautiful phrases—clear, distinct, concrete. For instance:

> "In the first hours of daybreak, the mind
> might comprise the World
> like the hand seizes a stone heated by sun."

This is from the first poem of his appraised debut collection. But in our context it was of no particular significance. Mainly because we have sun all-year round. And to us heated stones are just a part of everyday life, not a miracle as when Spring reaches Northern Europe. The deep meaning of the word "sun" wasn't within our reach. Furthermore, we experienced a constant awareness of fear, that prevented us from being able to wake up slowly and calmly. We woke up with the feelings from the day before, the same wrath and worries. My generation, born in the fifties, had no room for contemplation. Then and there we weren't able to accept the idyllic pasture. The fascination in dealing with it as a contrast to the man-made landscape was too subtle, arousing little more than indifference. In our cities there were no gardens. There was a constant noise giving no means to clearly single out a barking dog from the mass of sounds, thick as soot in our ears. We had loads of evil messages making us deaf to Tranströmer's peaceful moths settling themselves on the window pane as "tiny faded telegrams from the world".

Regardless, some of us could personally enjoy the skill of Tranströmer in making up expressions and images—for instance to describe silence:

> "Awake in the darkness one can hear
>   the constellations stomping in their stalls
>   high above the tree."

We started to find appreciation for Tranströmer's awareness of being a tiny person in front of the sea, or below the constellations in the midst of a dark forest. By this time Jorge Luis Borges was highly in fashion and for instance he had published an essay on metaphors and kennings of the Viking era literature, which was of great help to us in appreciating the Nordic poetry.

We could find the mythical substance we were looking for in phrases like:

> "Each person a door half open
>   to a room for everyone."

In due time the interest in poetry beyond political content arose; and Tranströmer grew closer to us particularly by his *private mythology*. By the phrase *private mythology*, I like to refer to the sentences and passages in which he alludes to the collective memory, illuminating the common origin and fate.

In 2011 the Mexican magazine La Otra published a selection of Tranströmer's poetry in translation by me and Lasse Söderberg. In an introduction the Editor wrote:

"We like to contribute to making Tranströmer's poetry better known, but to be honest it won't be as widely spread as other literary works by Nobel Laureates."

I don't necessarily agree with the statements in the editorial preface, but before the Nobel Prize Tranströmer wasn't published in Mexico in forty years or so.

KRISTIAN CARLSSON: Is it on account of his poetry being regarded as too "dry"?

ÁNGELA GARCÍA: Yes, both Lasse and I found it to be like that. The magazine quote illustrates one of the attitudes, not necessarily shared by the reading audience. I on my behalf have always been closely attached to contemplation—I was at once touched and terrified when I read Tranströmer's words about dusk and dawn:

> "Now the sunset comes creeping like a fox
> on this country."

And:

> "The Morning puts rays in the locks
> and the doors of darkness open."

This evokes the fear of all evils that creep and hide in darkness, but also the hope of miraculous keys opening a brand new day.

KRISTIAN CARLSSON: Here we have the darkness and the sun again, some of the familiar Tranströmer words Azita mentioned. But what about death, then? How is the Tranströmer perception of death perceived in a context where you are so closely affected by the presence of death?

ÁNGELA GARCÍA: Above all there is a few poems by Tranströmer made famous in Latin America. And those poems were carefully selected by his earliest translators, such as Paco Uriz. To begin with they selected poems with a political content that could make sense in the a Latin American context. The other side of Tranströmer's poetry came later, at a time when I had left the continent.

ANISUR RAHMAN: To find political relevance in poetry one should reflect upon the context of its origin. Tranströmer was born in 1931 and in 1936 Sweden became a welfare state. You can find Tranströmer's politics in his poetry, but it exists merely as a collection of experiences. From 1936 and onwards, and still in 2012, Sweden is a welfare state. Tranströmer lives in a time of welfare, and since writing is a loveletter to time, this has its effect on him. But in between we'll note our equal experiences in many of his poems. Still I agree with Ángela that he is representing the Swedish landscape, if not the Baltic landscape. And how is that landscape? As Azita pointed out, the method of poetical image in Tranströmer's poetry carries "Darkness", "Sun", "I", "Death", "Journey". In Scandinavia darkness and sun are very powerful elements in life and in nature. In Tranströmer we can realise the power of Darkness in wintertime and the importance of Sun in summertime. And from his first poems to his later poems all his writings are a single volume, from beginning to end, and this single volume is the beginning of a journey. If we go back to the first poem of his debut collection, he there addresses all the things he is going to say, it's the road map to life—and the destination is death.

ÁNGELA GARCÍA: My statement is precisely that we as readers face the conflict of different cultures and realities. When Tranströmer is talking about death or when he shares any political content—it always concerns the individual as a universal creature and not a person in the midst of difficult circumstances. He couldn't express the very concrete and harsh conditions of Latin American daily life. His poems reflects somewhat on the conditions of political reality, but not at all with precision in regards to world conflicts.

KRISTIAN CARLSSON: He wrote a lot from the point of view of a traveller. For instance he refers a few times to DDR (former East Germany) but his poetry never involves itself in the collective tragedy. It's more of a contrast.

ÁNGELA GARCÍA: He might have reached the collective, but not exactly in the sense of a situation in need of emergent attendance, he won't give any answers to be used as tools for the Movement. In the urgent situation you don't have time to understand the general questions about being an individual, there's a need for specific communication—regardless if you are able to grasp the content of other kinds of poetry or not.

ANISUR RAHMAN: One can also reflect upon Tranströmer's collection of letters to the North American poet and translator Robert Bly. The letters are also a kind of poetry, published under the title *Air mail*. They started corresponding in Swedish. Later on they wrote to each other in English instead. And in the letters you can find all the politically oriented notions of the contemporary world. And there you'll see how political he is.

AZITA GHAHREMAN: During my translations of his poetry I recognized him as a mystical poet, and he expressed himself as a philosopher too. When a philosopher talks about the world and his experiences and findings, and the exploring of the truth—he doesn't use the same methods as in usual literature. I think it would be better if we consider Tranströmer as a mystic and a philosopher. That fits better.

ANISUR RAHMAN: In fact I find his first poem to be the declaration of himself facing the world of poetry—beginning with:

> "Waking up is a parachute jump from
> dreams."

Thus he is jumping into another world, that is the world of poetry—and later on it shows that he is something, he is the Emperor or King of this world, jumping in a parachute, or you can say the Prophet is coming down from somewhere, from God. The declaration is so powerful to me, and I was still young when I first read it, and I was hypnotized by its power.

When I was a university student in Bangladesh at the turn of the century, I got familiar with very few Scandinavian literary voices. Hans Christian Andersen and Søren Kierkegaard from Denmark, Henrik Ibsen from Norway, and August Strindberg from Sweden. We weren't familiar with any contemporary Scandinavian literature. Then in 2005 there was a poetry reading in Stockholm where the Bengali translator Liakat Hossain was invited to recite contemporary poets from Bangladesh; some of my poems were in the program. At the event Tomas Tranströmer was a honorary guest, so when a report was published in a newspaper in Dhaka they also printed his portrait. That was my first notion about him, and then I also got an email where Hossain shared some many good words about the Swedish poet. A year later I had a Norwegian scholarship to translate Henrik Ibsen's poetry, and then some of my senior fellow poets asked me if I had also read the Swedish poet Tomas Tranströmer. I hadn't, but since I was familiar with the name, it created some curiosity in me—and I started to look for his books in the bookshops. I didn't manage to find any English editions, but there was a Bengali collection of Nordic poetry where he was included. Since I got disappointed by the translations, I decided to keep looking for English translations, which I failed to do even as I visited several Swedish bookshops when I was invited to Stockholm in 2006. That was a frustration to me. Back in Dhaka it only took some days before I was invited to the Swedish Embassy, but I had no clue to why they wanted to meet with me. So I met with the deputy head for a coffee, and at one stage of our conversation he gave me the collected poems of Tomas Tranströmer in English. He had brought the book back for me from a vacation in Sweden.

In Tranströmer I found the maddening power in constructing images. That made me run to finish the book, as if I had always been longing for those poems. At that time there was also discussions amongst the young poets, we were not pleased with the contemporary poetry. But now I was in charge of a powerful voice that would communicate my mind. In Tranströmer's poetry I found what was missing, and it was a very good reward to my hunger for reading poetry.

KRISTIAN CARLSSON: Is he well read amongst the poets of your generation, born in the seventies?

ANISUR RAHMAN: The serious writers are familiar with the name, and they try to read him in English; as that is our second language. But he isn't that publicly popular. Those who are expected to know, they do know about Tranströmer—this is the good thing.

When I first started writing poetry, senior poets explained that what is heard—the music or the rhythm—becomes the judging machine of the poetry. And it doesn't matter if Tranströmer's poetry is in English, Bengali, or Swedish—when I read it I find musicality that isn't dependant on any paticular language. In him I see a composer of musicality in the use of animating words, a master builder of images, meeting the spontaneity in the making of poetry. I salute him. I envy him. I am proud of him. And at one time after I had exiled to Sweden, I was asked by a friend:

"Have you seen the King or made a visit to his palace?"

I responded by saying:

"No, but I met with Tomas Tranströmer!"

TRANSTRÖMER
OUT OF LANGUAGE

To our knowledge we offer the first official translations of poems in Romani, North Sami, and Somali.

Poems in Bengali, English, Arabic, and the haikus in Japanese have been translated by our working group for this edition.

Poems in Farsi and Spanish are previously published translations that were made in collaboration with participants of our working group.

The previously published poem in Russian have been additionally compared to the Swedish original by our working group.

The poems in this section appear chronologically in regards to the Swedish editions.

Ur *17 dikter* (1954)
[From "17 Poems"]

/UPPVAKNANDET ÄR ETT FALLSKÄRMSHOPP…/
In previously unpublished Bengali translation
by Anisur Rahman (2012).

Ur *Hemligheter på vägen* (1958)
[From "Secrets on the Road"]

CAPRICHOS
HEMLIGHETER PÅ VÄGEN
In previously unpublished Somali translations
by Nimao Ahmed Bulaleh (2012).

Ur *Den halvfärdiga himlen* (1962)
[From "The Semi Sky"]

C-DUR
In Farsi translation by Azita Ghahreman & Sohrab Rahimi.
Previously published in *Roshanaye Tariki* (2012).

NOCTURNE
In Spanish translation by Ángela García & Lasse Söderberg.
Previously published in the Mexican magazine La Otra (2011).

Ur *Klanger och spår* (1966)
[From "Tones and Traces"]

KRÖN
In previously unpublished Lovari dialect Romani translation
by Iren Horvatne (2012).

Ur Det vilda torget (1983)
[From "The Wild Square"]

BLÅSIPPORNA
In Spanish translation by Ángela García & Lasse Söderberg.
Previously published in the Mexican magazine La Otra (2011).

Ur *För levande och döda* (1989)
[From "For the living and the dead"]

BERCEUSE
In previously unpublished Lovari dialect Romani translation
by Iren Horvatne (2012).

ROMANSKA BÅGAR
In previously unpublished Arabic translation
by Jamal Jumá (2012).

Ur *Sorgegondolen* (1996)
[From "The Sorrow Gondola"]

APRIL OCH TYSTNAD
In previously unpublished North Sami translation
by Simon Marainen (2012).

NATTBOKSBLAD
In Russian translation by Juri Gurman.
Previously published in *Traurnaja gondola* (1997).

TYSTNAD
In previously unpublished North Sami translation
by Simon Marainen (2012).

Ur *Den stora gåtan* (2004)
[From "The Grand Riddle"]

ÖRNKLIPPAN
FASADER
NOVEMBER
In previously unpublished English translations
by Kristian Carlsson (2012).

/HOPPLÖSHETES VÄGG.../
/TANKAR STÅR STILLA.../
In previously unpublished Japanese translations
by Hikaru Sugi (2012).

/STÅR PÅ BALKONGEN…/
/GLITTRANDE STÄDER…/
/RENTJUR I SOLGASS…/
In previously unpublished English translations
by Kristian Carlsson (2012).
In previously unpublished Japanese translations
by Hikaru Sugi (2012).

/BUREN AV MÖRKRET…/
/NOVEMBERSOLEN…/
/DESSA MILSTENAR…/
In previously unpublished Japanese translations
by Hikaru Sugi (2012).

/ALLÉERNA LUNKAR…/
/NÄR STUNDEN KOMMER…/
In previously unpublished English translations
by Kristian Carlsson (2012).
In previously unpublished Japanese translations
by Hikaru Sugi (2012).

/UPPENBARELSE…/
/MÄNNISKOFÅGLAR…/
In previously unpublished Japanese translations
by Hikaru Sugi (2012).

*

Uppvaknandet är ett fallskärmshopp från drömmen.
Fri från den kvävande virveln sjunker
resenären mot morgonens gröna zon.
Tingen flammar upp. Han förnimmer — i dallrande lärkans
position — de mäktiga trädrotsystemens
underjordiskt svängande lampor. Men ovan jord
står — i tropiskt flöde — grönskan, med
lyftade armar, lyssnande
till rytmen från ett osynligt pumpverk. Och han
sjunker mot sommaren, firas ned
i dess bländande krater, ned
genom schakt av grönfuktiga åldrar
skälvande under solturbinen. Så hejdas
denna lodräta färd genom ögonblicket och vingarna breddas
till fiskgjusens vila över ett strömmande vatten.
Bronsålderslurens
fredlösa ton
hänger över det bottenlösa.

I dagens första timmar kan medvetandet omfatta världen
som handen griper en solvarm sten.
Resenären står under trädet. Skall,
efter störtningen genom dödens virvel,
ett stort ljus vecklas ut över hans huvud?

*

জেগে ওঠা তো স্বপ্নের ভেতর থেকে
সকালের সবুজ দেশে মুক্ত পর্যটকের
শ্বাসরুদ্ধকর উল্লাসে প্যারাসুটে
                    লাফ দেয়া।
জিনিসেরা জ্বলে ওঠে।
শিহরিত ভারত পাখির মতে-
পর্যটক জানে বৃক্ষের ভূতলে ব্যাপক
                    শিকড় জংশন
        আর দোলানো বাতি বৃত্তান্ত।
কিন্তু ভূস্তরের সবুজ দারু-
মৌসুমী বন্যা
যেন তার উত্তোলিত বাহু
অদৃশ্য পাম্পের শব্দ চারু।
পর্যটক যেন গ্রীষ্মের দিকে
                পা মাড়ায়
দৃষ্টি সত্তা অগ্নিগিরির
            জ্বালামুখে নেমে যায়
যুগযুগের সূর্যের, সঞ্চালক চাকার
নিচে ভেজা সবুজ বৃক্ষের বাণের মাধ্যমে
                পর্যটক নেমে আসে-
এ যেন পরীক্ষিত, পতনমুখী ক্ষণিক যাত্রা

হুরমুড়ে চলা জলের ওপরে
বাতাসে ভেসে থাকা
বাজপাখির বাহাদুরী
পর্যটকের ব্রোঞ্জযুগের তুরী।
অচল নোট। অতল গভীর বাতাসে
ভেসে থাকা।
দিনের প্রথম প্রহরে স্মৃতিরা
দুনিয়াকে শক্ত করে আকড়ে
                টাকড়ে ধরে।

CAPRICHOS

Det mörknar i Huelva: soliga palmer
och tågvisslingens ilande
silvervita fladdermöss.

Gatorna har uppfyllts av människor.
Och damen som skyndar i trängseln väger försiktigt
det sista dagsljuset på sina ögons våg.

Kontorets fönster öppna. Ännu hörs
hur hästen trampar därinne.
Den gamla hästen med stämplarnas hovar.

Först efter midnatt blir gatorna tomma.
Det är äntligen blått på alla kontor.

Där uppe i rymden:
travande tyst, gnistrande och svart,
osedd och obunden,
med ryttaren avkastad:
en ny stjärnbild som jag kallar "Hästen".

CAPRICHOS

Mugdi bey noqoneysaa Huelva: geedka baarka ayaa iftiimaya
iyo codka tareenka oo degdegsan sida
fiidmeeraha oo kale, midabkooduna uu ahaa midabka dambaska.

Waddooyinka dad badan ayaa buux dhaafiyey. Iyo islaantii oo
degdegaysan dadka oo buuxa, ilayska maalineed uu sii libdhaya si
foojigan oo culays leh ayaa baardankuna indhaheeda uu saaran yahay.

Dariishadaha rugta hawsh wey furan yihiin. Hadana
waxaa la maqlaa ku tumashada dhulka sangaha oo socnaya.
Sange waayeel ah oo qoobkiisu samaynaya sumad.

Ka hor habeen badhka ayay wadooyinka dadku ka dhamaanayaan.
Kolkaas bey rugta hawsh noqdaan midab buluug ugu dambayn.

Hawadaa sare:
kadlaynaya si aan la maqlayn, widhwidhaya iyo madow,
lama arkaan mana xidhna,
gamaan fulihiina ka dhacay sangihiisii:
bilaabay xidigsi cusub oo aan ugu yeedho "Sange".

HEMLIGHETER PÅ VÄGEN

Dagsljuset träffade ansiktet på en som sov.
Han fick en livligare dröm
men vaknade ej.

Mörkret träffade ansiktet på en som gick
bland de andra i solens starka
otåliga strålar.

Det mörknade plötsligt som av ett störtregn.
Jag stod i ett rum som rymde alla ögonblick —
ett fjärilsmuseum.

Och ändå solen lika starkt som förut.
Dess otåliga penslar målade världen.

WADDADA QARSOON

Ilayska maalintii ayaa mid hurda fooda uga dhacday.
Qaraw isdabajoog ah ayuu galay
mase toosinee.

Mugdi ayaa mid dadka dhex maraya fooda uga dhacday
cadceeduna falaaro kulul
bay ganeysay oo salfudud.

Mugdi bey degdeg u noqotay sidii roob mahiigaan oo da'aya.
Waxaan taagnaa qol muggiisu yahay midaan maskaxdan ku qaban
karo dhamaantii kasoo ahaa guri lago kaydiyo balanbaalisaha.

Walina cadceedu sidi horebay u kululayd.
Burushka cadceeda oo salfudud baan ku rinjiyanayaa dunida.

C-DUR

När han kom ner på gatan efter kärleksmötet
virvlade snö i luften.
Vintern hade kommit
medan de låg hos varann.
Natten lyste vit.
Han gick fort av glädje.
Hela staden sluttade.
Förbipasserande leenden —
alla log bakom uppfällda kragar.
Det var fritt!
Och alla frågetecken började sjunga om Guds tillvaro.
Så tyckte han.

En musik gjorde sig lös
och gick i yrande snö
med långa steg.
Allting på vandring mot ton C.
En darrande kompass riktad mot C.
En timme ovanför plågorna.
Det var lätt!
Alla log bakom uppfällda kragar.

ماژور 3

بعد از عشق بازی تا به خیابان برگشت
برف در هوا چرخ می زد
زمستان؛ آمده بود
هنگامی که آنها در آغوش هم بودند
شب سپید می درخشید
او شادمانه تند می رفت و تمام شهر شیب داشت
رهگذران خندان می رفتند با یقه هایی بالازده
احساس رهایی و
همه ی علامت های سوال آواز سردادند در باره ی خدا
او اینطور حس می کرد
موسیقی خودش را رهاکرد
و با گام های بلند رفت در برف های چرخان
همه چیز در سفر سوی گام های «سی» بود
یک قطب نمای لرزان به سمت گام «سی» بود
ساعتی فراسوی تمام رنج ها
سبکبال بود
با یقه های بالازده، رهگذران ؛خندان می رفتند.

NOCTURNE

Jag kör genom en by om natten, husen stiger fram
i strålkastarskenet — de är vakna, de vill dricka.
Hus, lador, skyltar, herrelösa fordon — det är nu
de ikläder sig Livet. — Människorna sover:

en del kan sova fridfullt, andra har spända anletsdrag
som om de låg i hård träning för evigheten.
De vågar inte släppa allt fast deras sömn är tung.
De vilar som fällda bommar när mysteriet drar förbi.

Utanför byn går vägen länge mellan skogens träd.
Och träden träden tigande i endräkt med varann.
De har en teatralisk färg som finns i eldsken.
Vad deras löv är tydliga! De följer mig ända hem.

Jag ligger och ska somna, jag ser okända bilder
och tecken klottrande sig själva bakom ögonlocken
på mörkrets vägg. I springan mellan vakenhet och dröm
försöker ett stort brev tränga sig in förgäves.

NOCTURNO

Conduzco a través de una aldea en la noche, las casas surgen
En la luz de los reflectores — están despiertas, quieren beber.
Casas, graneros, avisos, vehículos sin dueño — es ahora
cuando se visten de Vida. — La Gente duerme:

unos pueden dormir plácidamente, otros tienen los rasgos tensos
como si estuvieran en duro entrenamiento para la eternidad.
No se atreven a soltar todo aunque su sueño sea pesado.
Descansan como barreras tendidas cuando el misterio pasa.

Fuera del pueblo sigue largo el camino entre los árboles del bosque.
Y los árboles los árboles callándose en mutua concordia.
Tienen el color teatral que hay en el brillo del fuego.
¡Cuán nítidas sus hojas! Me acompañan hasta casa.

Ya acostado voy a dormir, veo imágenes desconocidas
y signos garrapateándose tras los párpados
en la pared de la oscuridad. En el resquicio entre la vigilia y el sueño
una gran carta intenta deslizarse inútilmente.

KRÖN

Med en suck börjar hissarna stiga
i höghus ömtåliga som porslin.
Det blir en het dag ute på asfalten,
Trafikmärkena har sänkta ögonlock.

Landet en uppförsbacke mot himlen.
Krön efter krön, ingen riktig skugga.
Vi flyger fram på jakt efter Dig
genom sommaren i cinemascope.

Och på kvällen ligger jag som ett fartyg
med släckta lysen, på lagom avstånd
från verkligheten, medan besättningen
svärmar i parkerna där i land.

UPRUNIMO

Eke pharimasa len e liftura te vazdenpe
ande e uče khera, sigo phadjol sar o porslino.
Ek táto djés avela ávri po asfalto,
e dromeske tablenge jákha télej kerde.

O them ek opredromi e čéreske.
Uprunimo pala uprunimo, či sosko čáči šalin naj.
Ame uras ángle pala Tu
e milajeske cinamascopesa.

Taj pi ratji pašuvav sar ek hajovo
mundárde lámpenca, po dosta durimo
khatar o čačipe, mig e ekipi
mižal ande parkura kutka ando them.

BLÅSIPPORNA

Att förtrollas — ingenting är enklare. Det är ett av markens och vårens äldsta trick: blåsipporna. De är på något vis oväntade. De skjuter upp ur det bruna fjolårsprasslet på förbisedda platser där blicken annars aldrig stannar. De brinner och svävar, ja just svävar, och det beror på färgen. Den där ivriga violettblå färgen väger numera ingenting. Här är extas men lågt i tak. "Karriär" — ovidkommande! "Makt" och "publicitet" — löjeväckande! De ställde visst till med stor mottagning uppe i Nineve, the giordo rusk ok mykit bangh. Högt i tak — över alla hjässor hängde kristallkronorna som gamar av glas. Istället för en sådan överdekorerad och larmande återvändsgränd öppnar blåsipporna en lönngång till den verkliga festen, som är dödstyst.

* "the giordo rusk ok mykit bangh"
Citat ur Erikskrönikan (1300-talet),
beskriver musikutövning.

ANÉMONAS AZULES

¡Dejarse embrujar! — nada más sencillo. Es uno de los trucos más antiguos de la tierra y la primavera: Anémonas azules. De cierto modo son inesperadas. Brotan del pardo crujido del año recién ido en lugares inadvertidos donde de otro modo la mirada nunca se detendría. Alumbran y flotan, si flotan y es a causa del color. Este fervoroso azul violeta ahora no pesa nada. Es el éxtasis pero bajo techo angosto. "Hacer carrera" — ¡no viene al caso! "Poder" y "publicidad" — ¡risible! Al parecer organizaron una gran recepción arriba en Nínive, *the giordo rusk ok mykit bangh*. Alto en el techo — sobre todas las cabezas colgaban arañas de cristal como buitres de vidrio. En vez de un demasiado decorado y alarmante callejón sin salida las anémonas azules abren un camino de arces a la fiesta real, de silencio mortal.

---

* "the giordo rusk ok mykit bangh"
Cita de las Crónicas de Erik del siglo 14 que describe un ensayo musical.

BERCEUSE

Jag är en mumie som vilar i skogarnas blåa kista, i det ständiga
bruset av motor och gummi och asfalt.

Det som hänt under dagen sjunker, läxorna är tyngre än livet.

Skottkärran rullade fram på sitt enda hjul och själv färdades
jag på mitt snurrande psyke, men nu har tankarna slutat gå
runt och skottkärran fått vingar.

Långt om länge, då rymden är svart, ska ett flygplan komma. Pas-
sagerarna ska se städerna under sig glittra som goternas guld.

BERCEUSE

Me sim ek mumija so pihenij ande véšesko vuneto koporšovo, ande
savakutno e zajostar e motorengirestar taj e gumivostar taj dromestar.

Kodo so sas tela o djés téle žal, e lecki maj phárej sar o trajo.

I talička gurulindas ángle pe peski jékhutni rota taj me phiravadem
ma pe muro zalimasko psike, de akánik e gindura tordjile te žan
krujo taj a talička phaka kerdjile.

Dur pa butes, kana o oprunimo káloj, ek sastruni čirikji. E dromáre
dikhena e forura telape ke hodj čilogij sar e goterongo somnakaj.

ROMANSKA BÅGAR

Inne i den väldiga romanska kyrkan trängdes turisterna
    i halvmörkret.
Valv gapande bakom valv och ingen överblick.
Några ljuslågor fladdrade.
En ängel utan ansikte omfamnade mig
och viskade genom hela kroppen:
"Skäms inte för att du är människa, var stolt!
Inne i dig öppnar sig valv bakom valv oändligt.
Du blir aldrig färdig, och det är som det skall."
Jag var blind av tårar
och föstes ut på den solsjudande piazzan
tillsammans med Mr och Mrs Jones, Herr Tanaka och
    Signora Sabatini
och inne i dem alla öppnade sig valv bakom valv oändligt.

أقواس رومانية

داخل الكنيسة الرومانية الضخمة شبه المعتمة، ولج السياح.
قبو يتثاءب خلف قبو وليس من مشهد.
أضواء شموع رفرفت.
احتضنني ملاك لا وجه له
وهمس عبر جسدي كله:
"لا تخجل من كونك إنساناً، كن فخوراً!
في داخلك ينفتح قبو وراء قبو بلا نهاية
ولن تنتهي أبداً، هذا أمرٌ محتومٌ".
أضحيتُ أعمى من الدموع
وانقدتُ إلى الميدان المتّقد
برفقة السيد والسيدة جونس، السيد تاناكا والسنيورة ساباتيني
وفي داخلهم جميعاً ثمة قبو ينفتح وراء قبو إلى ما لا نهاية.

APRIL OCH TYSTNAD

Våren ligger öde.
Det sammetsmörka diket
krälar vid min sida
utan spegelbilder.

Det enda som lyser
är gula blommor.

Jag bärs i min skugga
som en fiol
i sin svarta låda.

Det enda jag vill säga
glimmar utom räckhåll
som silvret
hos pantlånaren.

CUOĐOMÁNNU JA JASKATVUOHTA

Giđđa vuoiŋŋasta ávdin.
Dat sevdnjesivnnat goivvodat
bonjada mu bálddas
speajalgovaidhaga.

Áidna mat báitet leat
fiskes lieđit.

Iežan suoivvan guoddá mu
dego fiovla
su čáhppes veaskus.

Áidna maid háliidan dadjat
šealgadit olletkeahttá
dego silbbat
pántaluoiki luhtte.

NATTBOKSBLAD

Jag landsteg en majnatt
i ett kyligt månsken
där gräs och blommor var grå
men doften grön.

Jag gled uppför sluttningen
i den färgblinda natten
medan vita stenar
signalerade till månen.

En tidrymd
några minuter lång
femtioåtta år bred.

Och bakom mig
bortom de blyskimrande vattnen
fanns den andra kusten
och de som härskade.

Människor med framtid
i stället för ansikten.

СТРАНИЦА ИЗ КНИГИ НОЧНОЙ

Майской ночью ступил я
в свет холодный луны,
цветы и трава были серы,
аромат же - зелен.

Я сползал в седловину
дальтонической ночи,
 а белые камни
слали сигналы луне.

Мир временной
был в две минуты длиною,
пятьдесят восемь лет в ширину.

И за мной в мире этом
за свинцово-тусклыми водами
поднимался тот берег
и тираны его.

Вместо лиц у тиранов -
великое завтра.

TYSTNAD

Gå förbi, de är begravda...
Ett moln glider över solskivan.

Svälten är en hög byggnad
som flyttar sig om natten

i sovrummet öppnar sig en hisstrummas
mörka stav mot innandömena.

Blommor i diket. Fanfar och tystnad.
Gå förbi, de är begravda...

Bordssilvret överlever i stora stim
på stort djup där Atlanten är svart.

JASKATVUOHTA

Vázze meaddel, dat leat hávdáduvvon...
Balva čierasta rastá beaivvášrieggá.

Nealgi lea alla visti
mii ija mielde sirdása

oađđinlanjas rahpasa hissabuohcci
sevdnjes soabbi siskkáldasaid vuosttá.

Lieđit luoddaguoras. Fánfára ja jaskatvuohta.
Vázze meaddel, dat leat hávdáduvvon...

Beavdesilbbat birgejit stuora joavkkus
čiekŋalasas gos Atlánta lea čáhppat.

ÖRNKLIPPAN

Bakom terrariets glas
reptilerna
underligt orörliga.

En kvinna hänger tvätt
i tystnaden.
Döden är vindstilla.

I markens djup
glider min själ
tyst som en komet.

CLIFF OF THE EAGLE

Remarkably immobile
reptiles
sealed by the vivarium glass.

A woman hanging laundry
by the quietude.
Death is windless.

In the depths of the ground
my soul glides
quietly as a comet.

FASADER

I

Vid vägs ände ser jag makten
och den liknar en lök
med överlappande ansikten
som lossnar ett efter ett...

II

Teatrarna töms. Det är midnatt.
Bokstäver flammar på fasaderna.
De obesvarade brevens gåta
sjunker genom det kalla glittret.

FAÇADES

I

At the end of the road I see the power
and it resembles an onion
where layers of overlapping faces
peel off one by one...

II

Theaters being emptied. It's midnight.
The façades have flaming letters.
The riddle of the unanswered letters
sinks through the coldness of tinsel.

NOVEMBER

När bödeln har tråkigt blir han farlig.
Den brinnande himlen rullar ihop sig.

Knackningar hörs från cell till cell
och rummet strömmar upp ur tjälen.

Några stenar lyser som fullmånar.

NOVEMBER

65

A bored hangman becomes dangerous.
The burning sky coils itself.

The knockings are heard from cell to cell
and the room flows out of the ground frost.

Some stones glow like full moons.

*

Hopplöshetes vägg...
Duvorna kommer och går
utan ansikten.

*

Tankar står stilla
som mosaikplattorna
i palatsgården.

この道よ
顔をもたない
鳩の群

モザイクの
パレスの庭に
佇めり

*

Står på balkongen

i en bur av solstrålar —

som en regnbåge.

朝の虹
三筋に光り
吾の前に

*

On the balcony

I stand in a sun ray cage—

just like a rainbow.

*

Glittande städer:

ton, sagor, matematik —

fast annorlunda.

輝きは
夫々にあり
街の灯も

*

In sparkling cities:

the tone, tales, mathematics —

although different.

*

Rentjur i solgass.

Flugorna syr och syr fast

skuggan vid marken.

トナカイの
影を縫い込む
地蝿かな

*

Sunbaked reindeer bull.

Flies sewing and stitching his

shadow to the ground.

*

Buren av mörkret.
Jag mötte en stor skugga
i ett par ögon.

*

Novembersolen...
min jätteskugga simmar
och blir en hägring.

君の目に
孤独を見たり
闇の檻

霜月や
影が泳いで
蜃気楼

*

Dessa milstenar

som gett sig ut på vandring.

Hör skogsduvans röst.

歩みいて
山鳩を聞く
一里塚

*

Alléerna lunkar

i koppel av solstrålar.

Ropade någon?

並木道
遠き呼び声
木漏れ日に

*

Trotting allée
leashed by bu
Was there a cl

*

När stunden kommer

vilar den blinda vinden

mot fasaderna.

時が来て
面に当たる
風が止む

*

When the moment comes

the blind wind will get some rest

against the façades.

*

Uppenbarelse.

Det gamla äppelträdet.

Havet är nära.

*

Människofåglar.

Äppelträden blommade.

Den stora gåtan.

海近し
林檎の古木
鮮やかに

人も鳥も
林檎の花も
謎に満ち

IN CASE OF
INSPIRATION FROM
TRANSTRÖMER

@ Kristian Carlsson

THE SOBER BOAT
English original (2012).
Previously unpublished.

@ Ángela García

VIAJERO
Spanish original (2012).
Previously unpublished.

VOYAGER
English translation by Kristian Carlsson & Ángela García (2012).
Previously unpublished.

@ Azita Ghahreman

NAAMEH
Farsi original.
Previously published in the magazine Rendan (2010).

LETTER
In English translation
by Maura Dooley and Elhum Shakerifar.
Previously published in *Selected poems* (2012).

[Swedish version available in *Under hypnos i Dr. Caligaris kabinett* (2012).]

@ Anisur Rahman

THE FEELING IN A NONSENSE READER
English original (2011).
Previously unpublished.

[Swedish version available in *Sex årstider* (2012).]

@ Kristian Carlsson

THE SOBER BOAT

Forgoing the collarless rivers
my crews cared nothing for my awes,
carrying by displacement
never to unload.

My waistline of breezes
and neckline of salt.
I take shoe size by
lower decks
on crossing ferries,
on crossing ferries.

Someone anchored
my leaf of grass
where undercurrent clouds abide.

@ Ángela García

VIAJERO

El vehículo detenido
abre un paréntesis de visión estática:
La aldea antes en movimiento
se recorta ahora contra el verdor.

Lo contemplado es agua para la inmersión del cuerpo.

Aprendiendo una fidelidad a la desnudez
la voz diseña el rostro oculto
en la apariencia de lo cotidiano
enuncia el deseo
contraste entre la vida sencilla
y el ardor de la imaginada,
donde el cuerpo bulle.

El vehículo es a la vez tiempo, viaje y camino,
recortados
contra la fantasmagoría de la vida tangible.

VOYAGER

The detained vehicle
opens a parenthesis of the static gaze:
Previously set in motion, the hamlet now
cuts itself out of the verdure.

The contemplation is water for one's body to submerge in.

Having aquired fidelity to the naked
countenance of plainness
the voice outlines a hidden face
by formulating desires;
a contrast of the simple life
and the ardor of imagination,
where the body burns.

The vehicle is at once time, voyage and path,
cutting itself out of
the phantasmagoria of tangible life.

نامه

سکوت خواب های زیادی دید
و به یاد آورد   شانه کسی را در خم آسمان
تو پرنده ای شدی با زخمی بزرگتر از سایه ات
وبه یاد آورد انگشت هایت را با آن رد کبود
بال های بریده کوچک در پاکت سفید
و به یاد آورد
چقدر ما خوب جنگیدیم
تا فراموشی مرگ را بغل کند

سکوت
مثل درخت ایستاده ای
هی سبز می شود   برگ می دهد
میو ه ها ؛ فانوس روشنی از خون
طولانی تر ازکلماتی که ما را کوتا ه برید
و خالی نوشت
در این تهی تیز است چاقوی تو
مثل گودال کنده در طول سال ها
پر از سیاه

سکوت راه را ادامه داد
ادا کرد ما را در خواب های بد
در این هوای گرفته و ابری پیچید دور ما
و آینه ی جیبی میان بری نداشت
تا باور کنی
باران از ابرهای تو   همیشه روشن تر است

LETTER

In the silence dreams came
and brought to mind   your silhouette against the sky
and you   changed into a bird   carrying hurt bigger than your
      own shadow
and this brought to mind   your cold, stained fingers,
those cut and folded wings placed in an envelope
and that brought to mind
how well we fought
to the bitter end.

Silence
in which you stand like a tree
putting out   green, unfolding leaves,
bountiful; a lantern glimmering with blood-red fruit
so much riper than
the sharp words that cut us short, hollowed us out.
In this emptiness
your knife is still sharp
it has gouged a pit in the passage of years
full of darkness.

Silence, in which we carried on,
making us act out bad dreams,
enfolding us in all those dark clouds,
proffering no handy little mirror for you to look in
and understand
that rain is brighter than   anything your clouds had to offer.

@ Anisur Rahman

THE FEELING IN A NONSENSE READER

At night when sleeping I dream, I wake up in the morning
Try to remember the dream at night, I want to see it come true in life
I want to remember and give frame to the images from dreams
By day when working I want to imagine the day as part of night
                                        dream

I want to have a feeling and draw some images as Tranströmer
                                        says
"Walking up is a parachute jump from dream." How I can feel it?
Who can feel it? Does Transtroömer feel it when a metaphor that
Shines true in him in Scandinavia, may not the same in Palestine!

I can make a long list, and I am sure his poems will lose many
                                        strong images
And metaphors in the war torn Afghanistan, Iraq, Africa and
                                        Middle East
To hunger run millions of children, women and the poor, homeless.
For whom sky is the roof and land is the bed what a big and
                                        powerful image it is!

No! Excuse me! Who am I to talk about a true genius like
                                        Tranströmer?
Who am I to talk about global economy, geo-politics, war and
                                        hunger?
I am nothing but a nonsense reader, I am nothing but a
                                        troublemaker—
Even in the true beautiful images in the poetry of Tomas
                                        Tranströmer?

Kristian Carlsson (b. 1978) is a Swedish writer, translator and curator of literary events. His first book was published in 1996, and he also writes original fiction in English.

Ángela García (b. 1957) is a poet, translator and curator of literary events. She was born in Columbia and now resides in Sweden. Her first book was published in 1993, and her poetry is now translated into several languages.

Azita Ghahreman (b. 1962) is one of the foremost contemporary poets of Iran, as well as a translator and essayist. She left Teheran in 2006 and now lives in Sweden. Her first book was published in 1990, and her poetry is now translated into several languages.

Anisur Rahman (b. 1978) is a writer and journalist from Bangladesh. He now lives in exile in Sweden, and was an ICORN guest writer 2009-2011. His first book was published in 2003, and he writes in both Bengali and English.